Farmer Frank and the Thieving Goose and other stories

2nd Letter to Emilee

CarolAnn Sanderson

 www.trafford.com

North America & international
toll-free: 1 888 232 4444 (USA & Canada)
fax: 812 355 4082

My Dear Granddaughter,

These are some of the stories I remember my Daddy, your Great—granddad Wilber telling me many, many times, even when I was in my twenties. Great-grandmother Wilber was his only wife. They were students in Pulman, WA, at the Washington State College, currently called Washington State University. They were married in February 1942, and in a short time they moved to the valley in King County, south of the cities of Seattle, & Renton, WA. They were asked to harvest the crops on the land that the Japanese farmers had planted and keep the land from returning to sand or being unusable.

Franklin Delano Roosevelt was the President of these United States. People were angry with Japan, and Our President used that anger and fear to order the internment of our fellow citizens in prison camps, and move farmers onto their land to harvest the crops left behind. On the Pacific coast, it was the Japanese. On the Atlantic coast it was the Italians and the Germans that were moved inland by the government forces.

I hope you get to know about my father, and why he was a special person as you read this book. He thought of his responsibilities to the animals on his farm or in his care much like you do. He was also caring for the other man's property so it was in better condition than when it was placed in his care.

Love in Christ,
Grandmother Sanderson

Daddy would always start off by Asking, "Can I tell you the Story of the night I had to spend time in the Hoosecow?"

My answer after I began to speak at age 18 months old was sure. And with a wink and a broad smile, he would reserve for when I was extremely good, and had all of my attention trained on his every word, then the story would come out to mommy's many, yet feeble protests, of "Oh Frank you do not want the children to know that you spent a night in Jail."

Glenn usually slept in mom's arms, when we were in the truck. Gloria wriggled in my lap as we sat between mom and dad in the old 1928 Modle T, Pick-up truck, which had the rear window for the cab missing. (Gloria is my sister 1 year and 2 weeks younger than me. Glenn is our brother 3 years, 2 months and 19 days younger than me.)

He continued, "My name is farmer Frank. I had bought 40 hens and 1 very happy rooster at auction for us. I had erected a pen with nesting boxes.

"One day in late Spring, after the threat of frost had long since past, I was out planting a row of corn, one seed at a time. The neighbor's thieving goose was hungry as the neighbor never took care, to feed his animals. So when I looked back to admire my nice straight rows, I saw this old mean gander toddling along behind uncovering a little over 1/2 the corn I had planted 1 corn kernel at a time, and so the goose was feeding himself, rather than allowing me the crops, I had expected for the fall harvest. (Because of the large amount of rain and sunshine there always have been, farmers in and around the Green and Cedar River Valley, who raised the largest part the food sold in roadside stands.)

I asked our daddy what did you do to stop the goose from eating his breakfast, dad?

Our dad replied, "Be patient little one. I did not want to hurt the Gander. (A gander is a daddy type goose.) So I made a pathway to the chicken pen of the same corn that I was using for seed.

The path led him into the chicken pen and while he ate, I closed the gate to the pen.

The pen was made of posts a little over 6 feet tall with small boards going between them to hang the wire mesh to form the walls, more chicken wire across the top to keep them from flying away. I had built a small house to one end in which the animals could take shelter from rain and wind. I always kept the floor of the coop and pen in clean hay. I fed my animals and their guests before I fed myself every morning. And the gander greeted me with the chickens every morning. A couple of days later the mother goose came over to my fields looking for her husband, and eating her fill of my grain which I laid down as a path to the chicken pen again and in she went to eat from the pile of corn that I had given her gander and my hens. We collected her eggs each morning along with about 3 dozen chicken eggs as there were always a couple of the hens that were on vacation each morning."

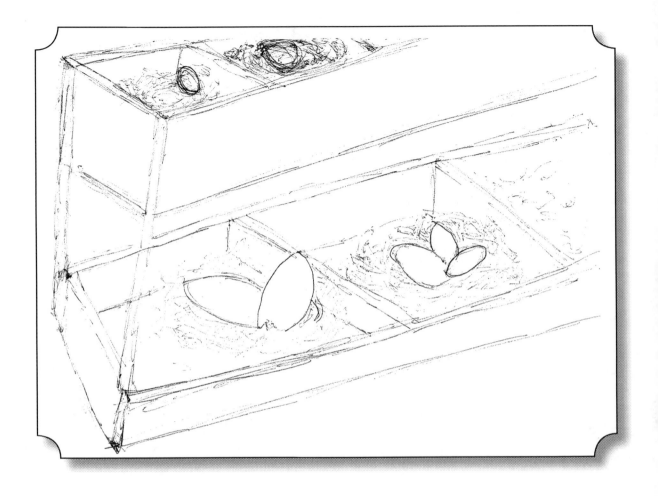

What happened then? I asked him.

"Well in short time my chicken pen had our chickens the neighbor's 2 geese, and his 6 ducks. I fed them daily, used their waist product in our kitchen garden as fertilizer, collected their eggs for eating, and bartering or out and out selling them. The neighbor knew that I had his birds, but never came to ask me for them, Yet, the Monday before Thanks Giving Day, he went to the sheriff, and complained that I had stolen his gander and that he wanted me to be arrested and his gander returned to him.

"I was asked by the Sheriff, 'Do you have your neighbor's gander, Farmer Frank?' To which I said that I did. The Sherriff took me in, telling your mommy that she could ask someone to help get me out. The judge would hear the case the next morning, but for that night unless we could pay my bail, I would be in jail. Your mommy called my mother, the pastor, & any of my friends who might be able to help. But there was no money for bail.

"The next morning I was awaken early and assigned a public defender, who never opened his mouth in court to defend me. He asked me before hand, if I had the gander belonging to my neighbor. I had tried to tell him why. But the lawyer did not believe me.

So the judge asked if I had the gander in question, to which the lawyer objected that I did not need to answer questions that might convict me.

I said I did have it, and explained that the goose was not being fed by my neighbor. He and his Mrs. goose and 6 ducks were all in with my chickens, being fed daily, and their shit being collected daily and eggs too. In exchange for this, I feed them and they have all been gaining weight. All he had to do was to ask me for them and I would have given them back, but he never asked. So the Judge asked me how many of the neighbor's birds were in with my chickens. I answered a pair of geese & 6 ducks.

"The judge then asked the neighbor, if what I said was true. He said, 'yes it was, but if the man was willing to feed my birds then why should I stop him.?'"

"The judge then ruled that 'yes he could have the Gander, but I could keep the mother goose & 6 ducks in exchange for the seed corn I had fed the birds .'"

Daddy was that the end of the story? I asked.

"No, dear, I paid the lawyer by a cheque and received a receipt for the payment. But I never filed them though I knew that I should have. So when the lawyer sent me a bill 6 months later, I sued to not have to pay the bill twice.

to Lawyer 50⁰⁰
Fifty ⁰⁰
defence Fee   Former Fr...

"The judge asked if I could produce either the canceled cheque or the receipt. I said that I could not find either, but wrote the cheque the day of the trial. But the judge had no choice but to rule that I had to pay the bill again, which I did. Now little girl, if you pay a bill at all never lose or destroy the cheque, and be sure to keep the receipt."

I wish to thank my brother-in-law, Dean Henry Fearn, retired professor of Computor analysis at Hayward University, who encouraged me to tell this story to him in a conversation, and after I wrote it down to have it published. As he thought it was funny but a good look into the personality of my father. Dean also edited this story for me.

My mother is no longer someone I can ask about my family history, at 95 years of age, but she has enjoyed being reminded of her only husband, as I read the transcript of this story to her. She remembers some of the history of their marriage, once you prime the memory so to speak. It is rather like priming a water pump, you have to pour in a memory or two so that can bring on other memories . . .

My father, Frank Albert Wilber died April 1, 1994 (just before his 72 birthday, having been born April 22, 1919).

This is the second in a series I call: "Letters to Emilee."

I hope you enjoy this book as it casts a light on small amount of the history of our country at war.

Story 2

You Can Not Win a War With a 1 Ton Cow

by

CarolAnn Sanderson

This second story in this book is also about my father, Farmer Frank of his farming when he first came to the valley. When the war was over, there were men who said they represented the department of the Interior through which he had been asked to care for his Japanese neighbor's farms. They asked him if he wanted to buy the farms he had been caring for? They were offering the land at a dollar an acre.

Farmer Frank said, "it is not your land to sell."

The men said, "yes it is. They will not return for it."

Frank said I will not be a party to the theft of another man's property."

So later that day when the first of the farmers who had left their farms came back, Farmer Frank welcomed him back to his farm. He showed the Japanese man the improvements he had made to the property.

Then Farmer Frank moved our family into the trailer he borrowed again from the minister. He bought a scant 1 acer from the big milk farmer who was on the West Highway. Then dad got a quancit hut from the army surplus store. He put it on the northern 1/3 of his lot. It looked funny with the gape in the middle. But that was before some used greenhouse windows that he bought from the nurseryman that he had purchased plants and soil amendments from for his new profession of landscaping. Those windows were used to tie the two haves together to make a house. Our house not only had those windows on either side but unlike so many in the 1940s. We had a sky light made of the same type of windows.

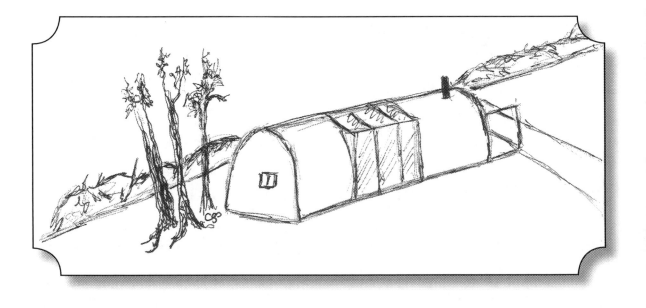

He worked on the other buildings: the barn, cement block garage, the hen house and chicken pen. Then Farmer Frank went to the Auction & bought a beautiful cow and the chickens that free ranged in our yard except when he was planting our garden. He had moved us into the quancit hut on the West Valley Highway just South of the Green River Bridge South of Kent, WA.

Father believed if you had an animal on your property, you should feed and water that animal before you feed yourself. I loved running after him as did his cat, while he was milking the cow, and collecting eggs from the chickens. I started following him not long after I could walk. It took three of my steps for each of his long strides.

Father got up at 5:AM every morning and took his clean bucket out to the little barn to milk the cow in the single stantion, the cat sitting on the lowest rail of the stantion fence watching the goings on. I peeked through the bars just watching what Farmer Frank was doing. He hung a bag of feed open for the cow to eat. on the fence in front of her. He had a can of hot water, disinfectant and a soft sponge.

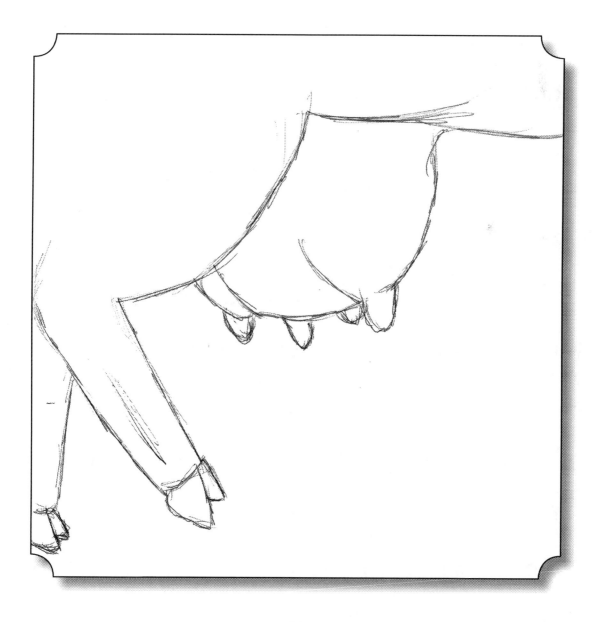

(The udder of a cow is the large bag towards the rear of the lower part of cow. The cow is a female bovine. I am of course, speaking of domesticated cattle. They are related to Deers and Bison or Elk.)

Farmer Frank took down the three legged stool from the hook on the rafter, sat it on the floor on the right side of the cow near the hind leg and Sat upon it stroking Blondey on her side, She and dad had a strange friendship, I thought, as he took the sponge into his hand, rang it out and inspecting the udder of the cow for cuts or scrapes he washed it thoroughly. Then Farmer

Frank positioned the pail which was a five gallon galvanized type, between his knees, and squeezing Blondey's tits, with the thumb under his fingers. The milk began to flow. He bent one of the tits to squirt some milk in the cats face, which made her first lick her lips then clean her face with her paw.

Blondey turned around to see why the difference in the sound of the milk in the pail. Then she raised her right hind foot, and stomped on my Farmer Frank's foot, just above his toes.

He pushed her away against the wall of the barn. In retaliation Blondey kicked him in the shin. Farmer Frank Hit her on her hip. I noticed Blood was running down one of his shoelaces.

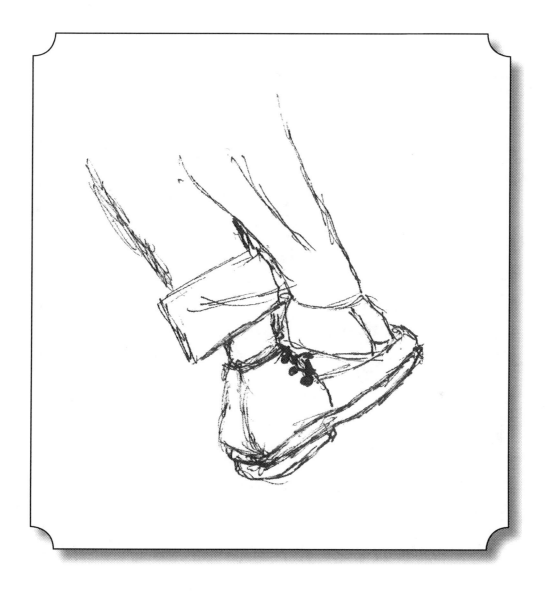

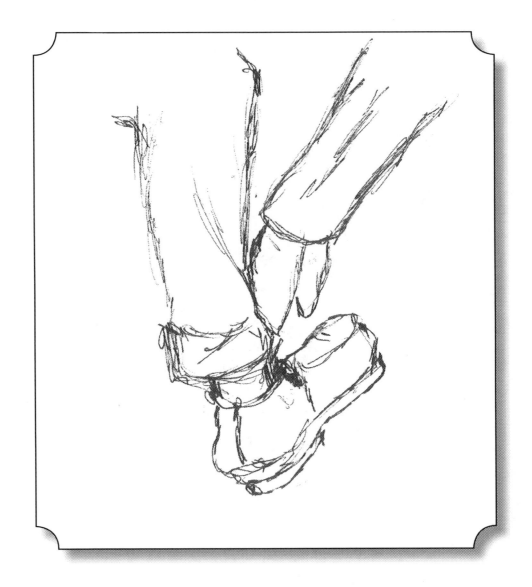

All the while, Blondey was eating from the bag that Farmer Frank had put oats in for her. He continued to milk Blondey. (She usually gave five gallons in the morning and another five in the evening. True to her breed of cow, she gave a large amount of butter fat, about 20%.). Blondey was a Gernsey of a light brown to yellow hair with big brown eyes.

She is smaller than the Holstines our neighbor down the road had. The Jersey was a little smaller than her. But dad wanted a cow that was sturdy and could last out in the floods that our area was known to be plagued. Farmer Frank was almost done milking the cow. When she was done eating, she picked up her foot and stepped into the bucket rendering it useless, kicked it over as she ran out of the barn. Farmer Frank picked up the stool & said to me, "little girl, don't you tell mommy what happened. Then he got a bucket of grain for our chickens. He poured it into the chicken yard for the hens and rooster to eat.

While the chickens were distracted, dad and I
went into the hen house and collected the eggs.
Daddy lifted the nesting hen's feathers and

I tenuously reached in my hand to get the egg hidden there. Though we had 40 hens we usually got 35 or 36 each morning. "There are always 3 or 4 hens on vacation, but never the same ones." So says Farmer Frank . . . .

After we collected the eggs, we took the eggs in the milk bucket which daddy had washed out. "Mommy asked what happened to the milk."

I held up the bucket for her to see the eggs we

had collected, and smiled with pride. Daddy had

taken off his boots on the porch, so he would not have tracked in mud, having already removed mine . . . When he came into the house, Farmer Frank said, "You cannot win a war with a one ton cow . . . . Do you want me to go to Smith Farm. to buy a gallon of milk?"

3rd story

Grass Is Always Greener

by
CarolAnn Sanderson

Dad had planted our pasture with Kentucky Blue Grass, Perennial Rye Grass and Fescue to which he had added Pink and white Clover. This should have made the grass sweeter to the cow's taste buds. But when dad was going to work on a garden he was installing in a client's home, Farmer Frank saw Blondey, the cow stretching her head through the wire fence to eat the dried up brown grass in the neighbor's yard.

The Farmer next door no longer had cows, thus Farmer Frank questioned if there was another reason for his Blondey to want to eat from the neighbor's farm. Yet on one day Farmer Frank took down the sythe telling me to go sit on the porch. Then he entered the pasture and started swinging the sythe cutting the grass on about 1/2 of the pasture. Blondey did not pay attention. Until Farmer Frank came back with a rope to tie her up to a fence post near the barn. Then Farmer Frank got the flat tined pitchfork and digging the barn out and into the manure pile to the back of the barn. Next he washed the floor with hose and broom. This is a chore that Farmer Frank did every evening.

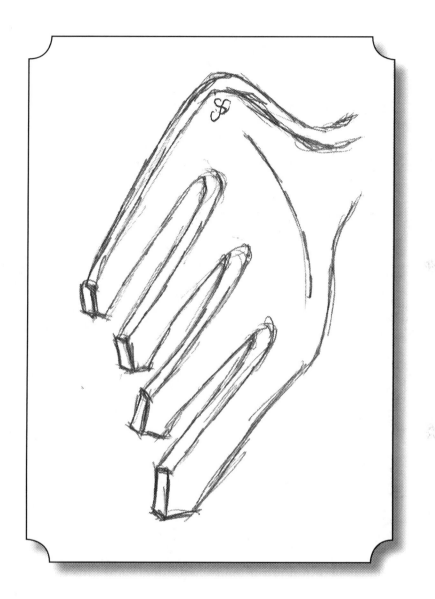

He got a scoop of the oats that he fed his cow
and put it in the feed bag that hangs on the gate
fence to be eaten from as he milks the cow then

he got the clean milk pail and the bucket of disinfecting hot water and sponge, placing them on the three legged stool. Then Farmer Frank got the cow and as she ate, He washed her udder and started to milk the cow while he sang to her. This time she did not fight him. Farmer Frank filled the five gallon bucket and turned Blondey out into the field. The months of June, July and August have weather that is drier south of Seattle. So if the cow would stay off of the cut grass for a couple of days, Farmer Frank could have some hay for Winter, which he put in the loft.

Every spring Blondey gave us a calf which we watched grow and play. But every fall it would leave our farm. One day late in August we had a phone call from the neighbor to the South of us. Blondey and her calf had been eating the neighbors grass stretching their heads through the wire until the fence section fell over. Now they were running loose. The neighbor would help Farmer Frank get them home so that they would not get killed by a truck as was our Golden Cocker, Queeny just days before. Farmer Frank sat down on the step outside, put on his shoes and took down the rope from the wall near the door. He walked to the neighbor's rope in hand. The neighbor, with the help of his children had the cow and calf cornered in the flower beds, where they had gone to eat blossoms.

"Frank, I thought you said that they would stay home after you planted the clover in your pasture."

"I expected them to do so. I was wrong. I will be tying them up until I get the posts replaced and the wire up. I am embarrassed that they went and ate your flowers. I will make it right for you as soon as I can."

The neighbor put a rope around the calf's neck and walked across the fence and field with Farmer Frank to a post near the milk barn. There they were tied up to keep them from roaming and being a traffic problem. Farmer Frank had some posts stacked by his garage to use for the gardening he was to do for his clients. He took two of them and planted them in the ground in the same holes used for the old fence poles and backfilled each with Portland Cement.

Blondey and her calf grazing from the neighbor's grass through the fence, Farmer Frank was told, by the old farmer down the street, who was his mentor. "There is nothing a man can do to make a cow realize that she is wrong. Blondey thinks the Grass is greener on the other side of the fence."

Farmer Frank was not going to give up. Quit was not in his vocabulary. He did not like barbed wire as it scratched cattle and other animals or people indiscriminately. (He always said that when you are fencing land you are responsible to see that your animals and other people are not injured. Yet that they stay where you want them.) The old Farmer listened to his younger friend, and then he said, I think you are on the right track. I will not tell you what you should do, because you will find the answer as you try the puzzle. You are a smart man, who thinks and reasons well. You will find an answer, if you continue the way that you are.

The next day Farmer Frank continued with looking for a plant that is not poison but is a good deterent to a cow stretching her neck through it to eat what she thinks looks sweeter than what she has in her own pasture.

Farmer Frank bought some seeds for horseradish and spread them under the fence, hopping that the smell would repel the cow. But the cow was not impressed. Farmer Frank watered those seeds every day until they were sprouting, each day after he cut the grass with the sythe, Farmer Frank turned the grass over so that the grass could dry out. When it had dried sufficiently, he put the hay up in the loft, above the milking stantion.

(A stantion is a small gated milking pen big enough to close in the cow, so she can be examined for injury or cleaned in the area of the udder). Then, milking is the next thing that was done.